HORSHAM TOWNSHIP LIBRARY
435 BABYLON RD., HORSHAM, PA 19044-1224

3 1224 1006 0623 4

P9-CDW-801

Withdrawn
Horsham Township Library

Horsham Township Library
435 Babylon Road
Horsham, PA 19044-1224

ADD and ADHD

Perspectives on Mental Health

by Judith Peacock

Consultant:
Catherine K. Lee
Certified Professional Counselor
Columbia, Maryland

LifeMatters
an imprint of Capstone Press
Mankato, Minnesota

LifeMatters Books are published by Capstone Press
PO Box 669 • 151 Good Counsel Drive • Mankato, Minnesota 56002
http://www.capstone-press.com

©2002 Capstone Press. All rights reserved. No part of this book may be reproduced or transmitted in any form or by any means without written permission from the publisher. The publisher takes no responsibility for the use of any of the materials or methods described in this book nor for the products thereof.

Printed in the United States of America

Library of Congress Cataloging-in-Publication Data
Peacock, Judith.
    ADD and ADHD / by Judith Peacock.
        p.   cm. — (Perspectives on mental health)
    Includes bibliographical references and index.
    ISBN 0-7368-1029-3
    1. Attention-deficit hyperactivity disorder—Juvenile literature. [1. Attention-deficit hyperactivity disorder.] I. Title. II. Series.
    RJ506.H9 P43 2002
    616.85′89—dc21   00-012936
                                                            CIP

    Summary: Describes ADHD and how this condition may affect teens. Discusses causes, diagnosis, and treatment of ADHD, as well as how teens can cope with, gain control over, and live with the disorder.

Staff Credits
Charles Pederson, editor; Adam Lazar, designer; Kim Danger, photo researcher

Photo Credits
Cover: ©Capstone Press/Gary Sundermeyer
Artville/Clair Alaska, 7, 8, 42, 49, 52, 53; Don Carstens, 13
Digital Vision, 35
Photo Network, 36/©Myrleen Ferguson, 15; ©Esbin-Anderson, 25, 29
Photri Inc/©Skjold, 20; ©Bachmann, 59
Pictor/©Llewellyn, 45

A 0 9 8 7 6 5 4 3 2 1

Table of Contents

ADHD stands for attention deficit hyperactivity disorder. Many people use the term *ADD*, which is also correct and stands simply for *attention deficit disorder*.

People with ADHD may have trouble sitting still, controlling their impulses, and paying attention. These behaviors can lead to problems at school, at work, and in the home.

ADHD isn't the same as mental retardation or emotional illness. Most people with ADHD are bright, energetic, and creative.

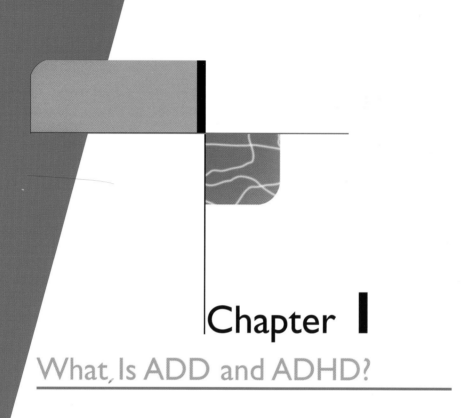

Chapter 1

What Is ADD and ADHD?

Do you know kids who seem to bounce off the walls? Their behavior may drive you and everybody else crazy. Maybe you know kids who never pay attention to anything around them. There may be an explanation for the behavior of these kids. The reason may be a medical condition called attention deficit hyperactivity disorder, or ADHD. (Many people use the term *ADD*, attention deficit disorder, which also is considered to be correct. This book will use *ADHD*.) You even may have this condition yourself.

Who Has ADHD?

From 3 to 7 percent of school-age children in the United States and Canada have ADHD. It's diagnosed, or determined, more often in boys than girls, although it occurs equally in both. ADHD affects children across all ranges of intelligence and ability. Most children with ADHD are of normal intelligence, or even smarter than average.

Symptoms of ADHD

"My little brother, Max, is 7 years old. This morning Max scattered cereal all over the kitchen. Then he stomped the spilled cereal to bits.

ISABELLE, AGE 13

"My mom told Max to get the dustpan and broom and clean up the mess. He got out the dustpan but forgot the rest of her orders. Within seconds, he was taking the dustpan apart. Was I ever glad when the bus finally picked him up for school."

The main symptoms of ADHD are hyperactivity, impulsiveness, and inattentiveness. A symptom is a sign of something else. In the case of ADHD, these symptoms are signs of a disorder. A teen with ADHD may have one, two, or all three behaviors.

Hyperactivity is a high level of activity. Children with hyperactivity have difficulty staying in one spot even for a minute.

Impulsiveness is acting without thinking. Teens with impulsive behavior rush headlong into any situation. They may interrupt others or grab things without asking.

Inattentiveness means not concentrating or paying attention. Inattentive teens can't stay focused on a task or an event, especially if it seems boring. Unimportant sounds or sights easily distract such teens.

One symptom of **ADHD** is an inability to pay attention.

Teens and ADHD

The symptoms of ADHD may ease up or change form in the teen years, or adolescence. Most noticeably, the hyperactivity of childhood may tone down into a restless, fidgety feeling. Some teens with ADHD may act sleepy. In school, they may tune out class discussions. Having ADHD can be especially hard for teens. They must cope not only with the ADHD but also with the normal stresses of adolescence.

"When I forget to take my medication, I feel like I can *FRANK, AGE 17* hardly sit still. And I act stupid. I'll know something is wrong, like shouting, but I'll do it anyway."

Is ADHD Real?

ADHD is a disability, just as being blind or unable to walk is. Teens and adults with ADHD, however, may not look disabled. They can be calm and quiet in an unfamiliar place. They also can spend hours doing something that interests them. These observations make people wonder if ADHD is real or just an excuse for poor behavior or performance. Doctors and scientists have shown, however, that ADHD is a true medical condition. It can have serious effects if left untreated.

The inability
of teens with
ADHD to do
well in school
can cause
serious
behavior
problems.

The Dark Side of ADHD

Teens with ADHD don't choose to be hyperactive, impulsive, or inattentive. In fact, they often try hard to do what other people want them to do. Without treatment, however, they may fail. Over the years, failure after failure can have serious consequences.

School and work. Teens with ADHD are likely to do poorly in school. Their inability to listen, follow directions, or complete assignments makes learning extremely difficult. They may decide to drop out of school because they can't keep up.

Social skills. Teens with ADHD may not know how to make friends with people their own age.

Family life. Parents may become frustrated and angry if the child constantly forgets chores or schoolwork. By the time the child is a teen, the parents may be ready to give up.

Safety. Their poor judgment and reckless behavior may put teens with ADHD in danger. For example, teens with ADHD get more speeding tickets than teens without ADHD.

Self-esteem. Teens with ADHD often may be scolded for their behavior. Low self-esteem can lead to alcohol and drug abuse, depression, criminal behavior, and other problems.

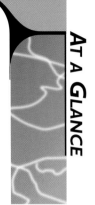
What's the difference between *ADD, ADHD,* or *ADD/ADHD*? All three terms really mean the same thing. According to the American Psychiatric Association, the "official" term is *AD/HD*. This term indicates that attention deficit can occur with or without hyperactivity.

The Bright Side of ADHD

In the past, people with ADHD often were labeled "bad," "lazy," or "stupid." They may have been beaten and shamed. However, having ADHD isn't all negative.

The symptoms of ADHD have been described through the centuries. Doctors and scientists today have a better understanding of the causes of ADHD. They know that having ADHD doesn't mean a person is bad. In addition, most children in the United States and Canada now are diagnosed at an early age. They can learn to cope with the symptoms before their life is permanently affected.

Most people with ADHD are creative and fun and have boundless energy. They often have the ability to think of more than one thing at once. In the right setting, these characteristics can be an advantage.

Points to Consider

What do you think when you see a child misbehaving in a store or other public place?

Do you know anyone who has been diagnosed with ADHD? What is this person like?

Why might it be difficult to have a friend with ADHD?

The exact cause of ADHD isn't known. Bad parenting, poor schools, head injuries, and too much sugar have been suggested. However, no proof has been found to support these ideas.

Most experts believe that ADHD has a biological rather than a social or psychological cause. The areas of the brain that control behavior may be understimulated in people with ADHD.

ADHD tends to run in families, which suggests a genetic cause in many instances.

People with ADHD often have other disorders as well, especially learning disorders. These disorders may be due to irregular brain function, or they may result from having ADHD.

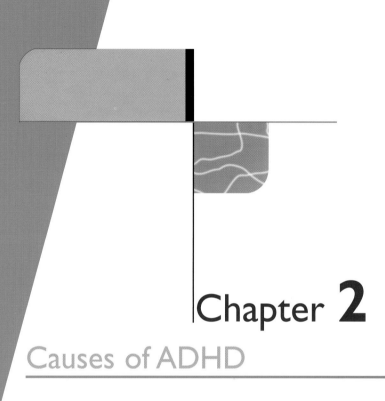

Chapter **2**

Causes of ADHD

Teens with ADHD may wonder why they have this condition. Were they born with it? Does something in their home or school cause them to be hyperactive? Did they learn impulsive behavior from their family?

Many causes of ADHD have been suggested in recent years. Some ideas have proven to be wrong. Other ideas are gaining scientific support. The exact cause of ADHD, however, remains unknown.

ADHD has had several names through the years, including *minimal brain damage, minimal brain dysfunction*, and *hyperkinetic reaction*. The name has changed as more is discovered about the disease.

What Doesn't Cause ADHD

During the 1980s and 1990s, the media paid a great deal of attention to ADHD. Books, magazines, newspaper articles, and TV shows promoted several theories about the causes of ADHD. These theories included bad parenting, poor schools, head injuries, and too much sugar.

Bad parenting. Parents don't teach their teens to be hyperactive, impulsive, or inattentive. Even the best parents may have teens with ADHD. Poor parenting and a difficult home life, however, can cause a teen's ADHD to be worse.

KEESHAWN, AGE 15

"Every year, parent-teacher conferences were the same. The teacher would tell my parents that I couldn't behave myself and always was causing trouble. My mom would start to cry, and my dad would get red in the face. The teacher never said so, but we could hear her thinking, 'What's wrong with these parents! Why haven't they raised Keeshawn to behave? All this kid needs is a dose of old-fashioned discipline.' I felt sorry for my parents. I know they did their best to raise me. I tried hard to behave, but I just couldn't seem to get it together."

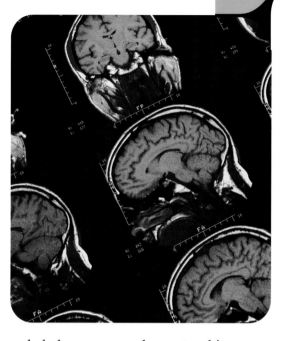

ADHD may be a type of brain disorder, but it is not caused by damage to the brain.

Poor schools. Crowded classrooms and poor teaching may cause teens to be restless and bored. However, poor behavior in this situation is not necessarily ADHD.

Minor head injury or damage to the brain. At one time, ADHD was called "minimal brain damage." This term is no longer used. Most people with ADHD have never had a head injury or an illness that affected the brain.

Too much refined sugar. Parents have been told to keep sugar away from teens with hyperactivity. Candy, soft drinks, and foods with artificial sweeteners and flavorings were said to cause a "sugar high." Sugar generally doesn't make teens hyper. In fact, the opposite may be true. Too much sugar may cause teens to be slow and dull.

Scientific studies have found little or no support for any of these theories. Even so, wrong ideas about the causes of ADHD continue to exist.

The National Institutes of Health (NIH) says that refined sugar may cause hyperactivity and inattention in about 5 percent of children with ADHD. These are mostly very young children or children with food allergies.

What May Cause ADHD

Scientists are finding more evidence that ADHD stems from irregular brain function. Brain scan images show important differences between people with ADHD and people without it. Certain areas of the brain control impulses, attention, and hyperactivity. People with ADHD appear to have a low level of activity in these areas. In other words, the brain isn't working as hard as it should to control these people's behavior.

Several reasons may explain this reduced brain activity. One reason may be inefficient use of glucose, a type of sugar the body needs for energy. Poor blood flow to parts of the brain also may relate to inactivity.

Perhaps the strongest reason is a lack of certain neurotransmitters. These brain chemicals help nerve cells communicate. Certain medications can stimulate the brain of people with ADHD. This supports the idea of a chemical deficiency.

"I have attention deficit disorder. The brain of someone with ADD gets flooded with information. Our brain takes in everything that comes along and then processes it in a disconnected way. A 'normal' person's thoughts go from A to B to C. The brain of someone with ADD goes from A to T to X, and back to A again. Having ADD can be very confusing."

HARLEY, AGE 17

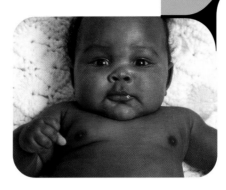

ADHD is almost always present at birth or develops shortly afterward.

Inherited vs. Noninherited ADHD

"My mother says I was restless even as a baby. I started walking at 7 months and never stopped moving. We couldn't have any knickknacks in our house. Nothing could be within my reach. I'd knock down anything I could get my hands on.

CHEYENNE, AGE 14

"When I was 10 months old, I kicked out the side of my crib. My parents had to put mesh roping over the top of my crib to keep me from climbing out. I could swing from the top bar of the crib and drop to the floor. I really was a little monkey."

ADHD almost always is present at birth or develops shortly afterward. Studies indicate that at least 50 percent of ADHD cases are inherited. Parents may pass on to their children genes that influence the brain abnormalities of ADHD. If a teen has ADHD, it's likely that other members of the teen's family also have the condition.

The other 50 percent of ADHD cases may be due to problems during pregnancy, delivery, or early childhood. For example, medications taken during pregnancy or lack of care before birth can affect the developing child. So can use of alcohol and other drugs. Infections and exposure to lead and other poisons can cause brain abnormalities in infants and toddlers.

"My doctor says my ADHD is because my brain is wired different from other people's. It's not wired wrong, just different."—Zach, age 13

ADHD and Other Disorders

People with ADHD often have coexisting problems or secondary disorders as well. These can make diagnosing and treating ADHD more difficult.

Coexisting Problems

Disorders that exist along with another problem are called coexisting problems. When something affects the brain early in development, it's likely that more than one brain area is involved. Problems that may coexist with ADHD include the following:

Learning disabilities. People with ADHD often have difficulty reading, writing, or doing math. This may be the case even if they have average or above-average intelligence.

Mood disorder. People with ADHD may have problems with anxiety, anger, and depression. Bipolar disorder, or extreme mood swings, often goes hand in hand with ADHD.

Obsessive-compulsive disorder. People with obsessive-compulsive disorder feel an extreme need to think and do the same things over and over.

Muscle disorder. Some people with ADHD experience unwanted muscle contractions called tics. These can range from simple eye blinks and head jerks to hitting or biting.

The word *deficit* means "lack of something." A budget deficit is a lack of money. An attention deficit is a lack of attention.

Secondary Disorders

Secondary disorders result from a problem. People may have emotional, social, and behavioral problems because of their ADHD. For example, people with ADHD may become depressed because they can't complete tasks or get along with others.

No Excuses

According to experts, ADHD is a neurobiological disorder. That is, it's built into the brain. It's part of who the person is, just like eye color. Even so, ADHD shouldn't be an excuse for poor behavior or a lack of self-control. People with ADHD and their families still need to cope with this condition. They can learn to manage ADHD just as they would any other disability.

Points to Consider

Why might parents feel relieved to learn that their teen has ADHD?

Why might it be important to find the cause of ADHD?

Imagine that someone tells you, "The fast pace of modern life is causing more cases of ADHD." How would you respond?

ADHD can be extremely difficult to diagnose. Its symptoms resemble those of other physical and mental disorders. Other disorders can coexist with ADHD, which complicates the diagnosis. No scientific test exists to confirm a diagnosis of ADHD.

The American Psychiatric Association has established criteria for diagnosing ADHD. A person must meet these criteria to receive an official diagnosis of ADHD.

Not all teens with ADHD are alike. Several types of ADHD exist. Symptoms within each type can range from mild to severe.

A health professional uses information from interviews, rating scales, psychological tests, and school records to diagnose ADHD.

ADHD is underdiagnosed in females. Many children are diagnosed with ADHD. Still, a person may not be diagnosed until later in life.

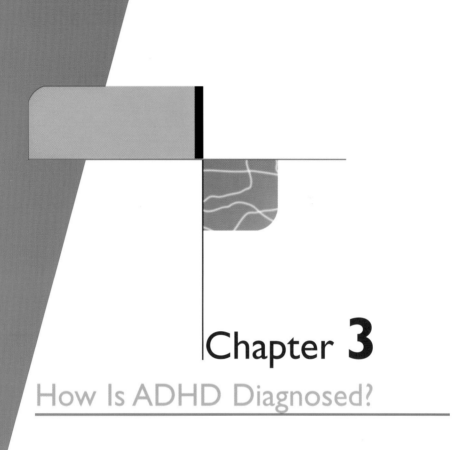

Chapter **3**

How Is ADHD Diagnosed?

"My intelligence is above average, but school always has been hard. I have seen many different doctors and specialists, but no one has had any solutions. Finally, I gave up—on school and myself. I started drinking a lot and doing drugs.

ELI, AGE 17

"The summer before 11th grade, my mom saw a magazine article on ADHD. It listed 10 symptoms. I had just about all of them. Our doctor diagnosed me with ADHD. I'm lucky I found out about my ADHD, so I could get the right treatment. But I wish I'd been diagnosed earlier. Maybe I could have done better in school."

The symptoms of ADHD sometimes are similar to symptoms of other disorders. It may be hard to tell if someone is depressed or has ADHD.

Is It ADHD or Something Else?

ADHD can be hard to diagnose. For one thing, the symptoms may be like normal, everyday behavior. Everyone is restless and fidgety at times, or can't concentrate. Being moody and withdrawn is often typical teen behavior. Younger children often are noisy and active.

For another thing, the symptoms of ADHD are similar to those of several other conditions. ADHD can be mistaken for other physical disorders. It can be mistaken for mental disorders such as bipolar disorder, anxiety, and depression. Other physical and mental conditions may coexist with ADHD. This makes it hard to tell which behaviors are related to ADHD and which aren't.

Finally, something at home or school might cause symptoms similar to those of ADHD. For example, a younger child or teen might react to physical abuse or divorce by acting out of control.

Because of these difficulties, ADHD easily can be misdiagnosed. Fortunately, however, health care professionals are becoming more skilled in diagnosing ADHD.

Standards for Diagnosing ADHD

At present, no scientific test is available to diagnose ADHD. No blood test or X ray exists that can prove whether someone has the disorder. Instead, an "official" diagnosis of ADHD rests on criteria, or standards, that the American Psychiatric Association (APA) has developed. Health care professionals must rely on their own skill and experience to determine if a person meets these criteria. The symptoms:

Must occur in two or more settings to be sure that not only the surroundings are causing the behavior.

Must have existed at least six months before diagnosis to be sure that a recent event hasn't caused the behavior.

Must have existed before age 7. Symptoms that begin after that age likely aren't ADHD.

Must interfere with the child's everyday functioning in school, at home, and among people.

Must be more frequent and severe than is normal for the level of development.

Researchers are trying to determine if the different types of ADHD are really separate disorders. If they're separate, methods of diagnosis and treatment might change.

Types of ADHD

Health care professionals generally diagnose ADHD as one of three types. Being more specific aids in planning treatment. The diagnosis is based on which behaviors occurred most often during the six months before diagnosis. Cases of ADHD can range from mild to severe within each type.

Primarily inattentive. The person shows more inattentiveness than hyperactivity or impulsiveness.

Primarily impulsive and hyperactive. The person shows more impulsiveness and hyperactivity than inattentiveness.

Combined. The person shows a significant amount of inattentiveness, impulsiveness, and hyperactivity.

Who Can Diagnose ADHD?

Parents and teachers might suspect that a teen has ADHD. Just suspecting ADHD, however, doesn't make it certain. A health professional with experience in diagnosing ADHD must give an official diagnosis. The following health professionals can diagnose ADHD.

A family doctor or pediatrician might observe symptoms of ADHD in a person. A pediatrician is a doctor who specializes in treating children. The doctor or pediatrician may do the assessment. Or the doctor may refer the person to a psychiatrist, psychologist, neurologist, or mental health worker for diagnosis.

A psychiatrist is a mental health doctor who can prescribe medication. Medication often is used to treat ADHD. Some psychiatrists specialize in working with children and teens.

A psychologist is trained to administer diagnostic tests and to counsel people. A psychologist is not a medical doctor.

A neurologist is a medical doctor who specializes in disorders of the brain and nervous system.

A mental health worker might be a social worker or psychiatric nurse trained to diagnose ADHD.

Biofeedback is being studied as a treatment for ADHD. This treatment teaches a person with ADHD to change his or her brain wave pattern.

Steps in Diagnosis

Health care professionals can't diagnose ADHD just by observing someone in their office. People with ADHD generally won't show typical behaviors in this setting. Instead, health care professionals gather information about the person from interviews. They also gather information from rating scales and questionnaires, psychological tests, and school records. A thorough diagnosis may take weeks or months.

Parent interview. A health professional asks parents to describe the teen's symptoms and when they first appeared. The interviewer also asks about other family members who show similar symptoms.

Teen interview. The teen describes how he or she gets along at home, at school, and with other people.

Rating scales and questionnaires. Parents and teachers answer questions on rating scales and questionnaires about the teen's behavior in various situations.

Psychological tests. Health professionals measure the teen's intelligence and school achievement using special tests. Teens with undiagnosed ADHD frequently fail to measure up to their ability.

School records. Report cards, teacher comments, and other school records provide valuable information.

Physical examination. A physical examination helps doctors rule out physical causes for the teen's symptoms.

Underdiagnosis of ADHD in Females

ADHD is diagnosed three to six times more often in boys than in girls. However, this doesn't mean that ADHD is more common in males. Many experts believe that ADHD may be underdiagnosed in females. Here's why.

Girls with ADHD tend to be primarily inattentive. In school, they're often the quiet daydreamers, so teachers may not notice their condition. Boys with ADHD tend to be more hyperactive and impulsive than girls. They tend to disrupt class and cause problems for teachers. Their ADHD may be discovered if teachers refer them for testing to find the cause of the misbehavior.

Some people think that too many teens are diagnosed with ADHD. They wonder if ADHD is just a medical fad. The American Medical Association (AMA) and the Centers for Disease Control and Prevention (CDC) don't think so. They say that more individuals are being diagnosed because parents and teachers are more aware of the symptoms of ADHD.

"My teachers always thought I was so sweet. They didn't notice that I couldn't sit still, had trouble concentrating, and ignored directions. But my mom was convinced I had a problem. She had the same behaviors when she was in school. She didn't want me to struggle the way she did. She finally took me to a doctor, who said I was smart but that I had ADHD."

KATELYN, AGE 13

Teens With Undiagnosed ADHD

About 70 percent of cases of ADHD now are diagnosed before the children become teens. Nevertheless, children with ADHD still may reach high school without being diagnosed. Why does this happen?

Most people link ADHD with hyperactivity. As mentioned earlier, not all teens are hyperactive. Teens with ADHD may disguise their disability in elementary school, especially if they're bright. Some teens with ADHD simply "fall through the cracks." This may happen because of overcrowded classrooms, misdiagnosis, or lack of knowledge about the disorder.

Teens who think they might have ADHD should ask a parent or school counselor to help them get tested. They might keep a list of their symptoms, along with examples. This information will help a health care professional make a correct diagnosis.

Could You Have ADHD?

If you answer yes to six or more of these questions, you might want to talk with your school counselor.

Do you feel like you're not getting anything done?

Are you easily frustrated?

Do you overreact emotionally or have temper tantrums?

Do you make so many careless mistakes with your schoolwork that it's affecting your grades?

Do family, friends, and others accuse you of not listening to them?

Do people comment on how you constantly drum your fingers, twirl your hair, or pace the room?

Are your desk, locker, and bedroom cluttered?

Do you put off doing things no matter what the task or how soon the deadline?

Do you daydream when you should be listening?

Do you blurt out things when others are talking?

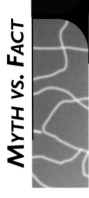

MYTH VS. FACT

Myth: All teens with ADHD are hyperactive.

Fact: Teens who are primarily inattentive actually may seem tired and slow moving. Some teens have a milder form of ADHD, and their hyperactivity isn't as noticeable. By the teen years, hyperactivity often is replaced by restlessness.

Do people call you "Motor Mouth" or say you talk too much?

Do you constantly change TV channels?

Do you begin doing something before reading or hearing the instructions?

Do you feel like your head is going to explode when you have several things to do?

Did you have trouble working your way through this list?

People with **ADHD** often live and work in cluttered, disorganized areas.

Points to Consider

Does every child who consistently is hyperactive have ADHD? Explain.

Imagine you think you or a friend might have ADHD. What should you do?

How would you feel about going to a mental health professional for testing?

Chapter Overview

Treatment for ADHD seeks to control hyperactivity, impulsiveness, and distractibility. Several methods may help to achieve this goal. ADHD can be difficult to treat if other problems are present.

Most effective treatment programs for ADHD include medication. Ritalin and other medicines help to regulate brain chemicals. Often, the use of drugs to treat hyperactivity has been controversial.

Behavior modification, counseling, skills training, and coaching teach people with ADHD how to manage their symptoms.

Adaptations in the home, school, or workplace can make daily living easier for people with ADHD.

People have suggested other treatments for ADHD. Little or no scientific evidence exists to prove the benefit of these treatments.

Chapter 4

Treatment of ADHD

Today, ADHD can't be cured, but it can be managed. Treatment for ADHD can include medication, education, counseling, and changes in the environment. The approach selected depends on the person's symptoms and age. Family members and teachers should be involved in the treatment program of a teen with ADHD. Any coexisting conditions also must be treated.

Medication
Medication usually is the main method for treating ADHD. It helps most people with the condition to calm down, concentrate better, and control their impulses. This helps them function better in everyday life.

In Canada, the use of Ritalin increased 637 percent from 1988 to 1998. In the United States, the number of prescriptions for Ritalin and other stimulants jumped 400 percent during the 1990s.

"I didn't know what normal concentration and attention were until I started taking Ritalin. It was like when I got glasses. I didn't know how bad my vision was until I put on my new glasses. Suddenly, I could see the leaves on trees and blades of grass. It was amazing!"

SLOANE, AGE 15

Types of Medication

Two main types of drugs used to treat ADHD are stimulants and antidepressants. As mentioned, scientists strongly suspect that a lack of neurotransmitters available in the brain causes ADHD. Stimulants cause two of these neurotransmitters, norepinephrine and dopamine, to last longer. Methylphenidate is a well-known stimulant for treating ADHD. Some brands of stimulants are Ritalin, Dexedrine, Cylert, and Adderall.

Antidepressants are used when stimulants don't work or when they result in unmanageable side effects. Antidepressants don't control hyperactivity, impulsiveness, and inattentiveness as well as stimulants do. However, they don't have to be taken as often as stimulants. Imipramine is a well-known antidepressant for treating ADHD.

Some people wonder how a stimulant can calm down someone with ADHD. Ritalin, for example, helps the nerves in the brain to conduct certain chemicals that help the brain work better. In turn, this improves the concentration of someone with ADHD.

Like all drugs, medications for ADHD produce side effects. Loss of appetite and sleep problems are the most common of these unwanted reactions to stimulants. Medications also may cause headaches, rapid heartbeat, and a feeling of sickness. Some teens become moody and irritable as the medication wears off. Changing the dosage or switching medications usually helps to relieve troublesome side effects.

Pros and Cons of Medication

The use of drugs to treat the symptoms of ADHD has been controversial, although less so today than in the past. Many people don't like the idea of giving drugs to younger children and teens. These people believe that parents and teachers may see drugs as a way to control inconvenient, difficult behavior. Also, drug therapy may give teens the idea that they can solve all their problems with a pill. Critics of drug therapy worry about the long-term effects of Ritalin. They worry that teens who take drugs for ADHD may start to use street drugs, as well.

Supporters of drug therapy say that taking Ritalin is no different than taking antibiotics for pneumonia. About 70 to 90 percent of teens who have been correctly diagnosed with ADHD respond well to medications. Ritalin has been used widely since the 1960s and has been proven safe during all that time. Finally, Ritalin and other drugs help teens cope with ADHD. This makes them less likely to use street drugs to feel better.

Education and Counseling

Even people with ADHD who do well on medication need help to modify their behavior. They also need a lot of encouragement. Behavior modification, counseling, skills training, and coaching can teach people with ADHD to be more in control of their behavior. These people learn to act in more socially accepted ways and be more productive.

Behavior Modification

Behavior modification uses rewards and punishments to change behavior. A teen with ADHD receives a reward if he or she does as a parent or teacher wants. This might be praise, a hug, a privilege such as TV time, or something material such as money. If the teen with ADHD does something inappropriate, parents or teachers might withhold privileges or restrict activities. For example, grounding is a common way to let teens know they have broken family rules.

If behavior modification works, then acting in appropriate ways becomes a habit. The teen won't expect or need a reward or punishment from parents or teachers. The teen often feels good about achieving more self-control.

Some parents use money or other privileges to motivate their teen with **ADHD**.

Counseling

Ongoing visits with a mental health professional can be an important part of treating ADHD. Older teens especially may benefit from counseling. It can help them understand ADHD and deal with their feelings of anger and depression. It can teach them problem-solving strategies and other ways to cope.

Since ADHD often creates conflict in families, counseling can help family members, too. Parents, for example, can learn effective ways to deal with their teen's symptoms. Counseling can be done individually or in groups.

> "I had mixed feelings about my brother's ADHD. On one hand, I felt guilty because he had all these problems and I didn't. On the other hand, I resented him because my parents were easier on him than on me. I hated the way he upset everyone and made our home a battleground. Family therapy helped me get my feelings out and showed my parents that ADHD was affecting me, too."
>
> ROBERTA, AGE 16

Coaching involves one-on-one work with a teacher or other person.

Skills Training

Classes or groups that teach skills for daily living are another way to help people with ADHD. Teens might participate in classes on anger management, memory skills, or study habits. They might join a group that teaches teens how to get along with peers. Local schools, community centers, or organizations for teens and adults with ADHD often sponsor skills training.

Coaching

Coaching is another way of learning to modify behavior. People with ADHD work one-on-one with a coach. This person teaches them to manage their time, organize and stick to a task, or solve problems. The coach might be a family member, teacher, teacher's aide, counselor, friend, coworker, or boss. Often, adults hire a coach.

Changing the Environment

The home, school, or work environment can affect the behavior of people with ADHD. For example, a noisy, disorganized classroom or workplace can increase hyperactivity. Changing the environment can help people with ADHD function better. Chapters 5, 6, and 7 provide examples of such accommodations.

Methods such as earning stars on a chart can reinforce positive behavior in younger children with ADHD. Teens with ADHD often respond well to written contracts with teachers and parents.

Alternative Therapies

Alternative therapies are treatments that may help a small number of people with ADHD. However, no scientific evidence proves their effectiveness. Health professionals who treat ADHD usually don't recommend alternative therapies as treatment for ADHD. Examples of alternative therapies for ADHD include the following:

Taking large amounts of vitamins

Avoiding certain foods, especially those with artificial flavors and colors

Eating herbs

Exercising different muscle groups

Points to Consider

How might you respond if a friend didn't want to take medications to control his or her ADHD?

Do you think behavior modification can work with teens? Explain.

Why might a teen object to going to a psychiatrist? What might you say to overcome the teen's objections?

Without help, teens with ADHD are likely to have difficulty in school. Poor school performance can lead to poor grades, losing self-esteem, and skipping school.

U.S. laws guarantee students with disabilities the right to a free and appropriate public education. Teens with ADHD may be eligible for special services under these laws.

Some teens have behavior problems linked to their ADHD. U.S. laws regulate appropriate ways to discipline these students.

Modifying the regular classroom can make learning easier for students with ADHD. Teens with ADHD and their parents need to seek and use accommodations.

Students can take advantage of many classroom modifications.

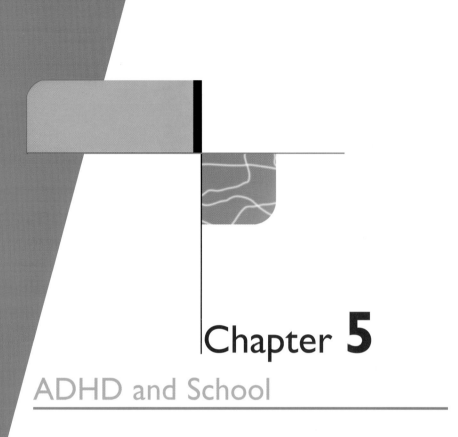

Chapter **5**

ADHD and School

School can be the most difficult situation teens with ADHD will face in their entire lifetime. Schools usually require students to sit still, listen, follow directions, and complete assignments quickly. These are all things many teens with ADHD find hard to do. In addition, many of these students have learning disabilities, which can make schoolwork even more difficult.

Fortunately, help is available. Schools, teachers, students, and parents can work together so teens with ADHD get a good education.

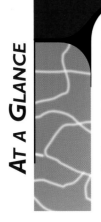

Middle school and high school may be harder than elementary school for students with ADHD. Students in higher grades must deal with different teachers and more homework. Teachers with large classes may not be able to give individual attention to students needing help. Students are expected to have certain basic skills when they reach high school. But students with ADHD may have gaps in their knowledge due to lack of attention and concentration in elementary school.

ADHD and the Law

In the United States, national laws guarantee individuals with disabilities a free and appropriate public education. Any school that receives money from the U.S. government must follow these laws. Two main laws are the Individuals With Disabilities Education Act (IDEA) and Section 504 of the Rehabilitation Act of 1973 (RA). Similar laws exist in Canada. Teens with ADHD may use these laws to seek educational services that meet their needs.

Individuals With Disabilities Education Act

Teens may receive special education services under the IDEA if their ADHD hinders their schoolwork or behavior. If they are eligible, then the school must provide them with an individualized education program. A team of individuals, which includes the teen's teachers and parents, writes the education program. It says how the school will meet the student's unique needs.

Section 504 of the Rehabilitation Act of 1973

Teens may receive services under the RA if their ADHD limits a major life activity. The act considers learning to be a major life activity, so teens with ADHD may qualify. If so, the school must provide a plan to meet their needs, in this case a 504 Accommodation Plan.

"When I do math problems, I tend to skip over the plus and minus signs. Now my teacher has me highlight the signs before I begin. This slows me down and makes me pay attention so I make fewer mistakes."
—Wally, age 14

The education and rehabilitation acts seem similar, but there are differences. Eligibility requirements are broader under the RA, so more students may receive services. The RA covers technical schools, colleges, and universities. The IDEA, however, is good through high school only.

Other Rights for Students With ADHD

In addition to a free and appropriate education, teens with ADHD have other rights under the law. These rights relate to extracurricular activities and school discipline.

Extracurricular activities. Most students enjoy extracurricular activities such as sports, band, or clubs. These activities also can help develop various skills and boost self-esteem. However, some students may not be able to participate because of low grades. This may include students with ADHD. Under the law, eligibility for students with disabilities can't be based on grades without considering the disability.

School discipline. Students with ADHD may be impulsive and easily angered or frustrated. These students may fight with classmates or talk back to teachers. Such students may be suspended or expelled from school. Suspension or expulsion may be inappropriate when the behavior is linked to a student's disability. The IDEA in particular provides safeguards to help determine how to discipline a student with special needs.

Studying in a modified classroom can make a positive difference for many students with ADHD.

Modifying the School Environment

Schools can modify the regular classroom to meet the needs of teens with ADHD. Here are some examples.

Provide a structured classroom. A structured classroom helps students with ADHD know what to expect.

Allow for flexibility. The teacher may bend rules occasionally if that will help the student with ADHD succeed. This might mean allowing the student to turn an assignment in late or allowing more time on a test.

Present information in an interesting way. Teens with ADHD are more likely to pay attention if lessons are lively and colorful.

Keep directions brief and simple. The teacher may number the directions as step 1 and so forth. Writing the steps on the chalkboard may make them clearer.

ADD and ADHD

Provide signals to help stay on track. For example, a teacher may place a hand on the student's shoulder. This tells the student it's time to settle down and start to work.

Assign a desk away from distractions. Sights and sounds coming from a window or door might distract a teen with ADHD.

Provide adaptations for learning disabilities. Students with ADHD might be allowed to use a calculator or to tape-record lecture notes.

What You Can Do

Students with ADHD should seek and take advantage of classroom modifications. Students can do many other things to help themselves be more successful in school. If you're a teen with ADHD, you already may have several ideas. Compare your ideas with the following list.

Take your medication when doing schoolwork. You'll be able to concentrate better and work more efficiently.

Arrange your class schedule to meet your needs. Ask to have your hardest classes in the morning before your medication wears off.

Organize your schoolwork. Write down assignments in a small notebook. Write on a calendar when major projects are due.

Some teens with ADHD study better with the TV or radio on. The noise helps block out other distractions. This sort of noise is called white noise.

Accept help. Ask someone you trust to proofread your assignments for careless mistakes.

Have a routine at home for getting your schoolwork done. Ask your family to help you stick to your schedule.

Learn and practice techniques for improving your schoolwork. For example, reading your work aloud or highlighting instructions before you begin may help you catch mistakes.

"I take Ritalin for my ADHD. It helps, but I've also learned skills to help myself. For example, I discovered that if I say things out loud, I remember them better. At home, I tell my mom what I need to do that day. At school, I repeat the teacher's directions for an assignment. I've also learned to use a computer for my reports. When I write things by hand, I get distracted by how hard it is for me to write. With the computer, my fingers can keep up with my thoughts."

HENRY, AGE 14

Some students with **ADHD** have trouble writing clearly. Being able to use a computer for writing assignments is often helpful for these students.

Points to Consider

What teaching methods help you learn best? What kind of classroom environment do you like?

What suggestions do you have to help a teen with ADHD do well in school?

What can parents do to help their teen with ADHD succeed in school?

Most teens dislike being singled out for special help or treatment. How can schools help students with ADHD without embarrassing them?

Teens with ADHD can take responsibility for managing their symptoms.

Recognizing strengths as well as weaknesses is important. Teens who feel good about themselves will want to take charge of their life. Getting more involved in their treatment program is an important way to take charge.

Teens with ADHD who are in control of their behavior speak up for themselves. They tell teachers, parents, and others what they need and what works for them. They also practice good health habits.

Teens with ADHD may need to control a tendency to act without thinking. Impulsiveness can damage friendships and even endanger lives.

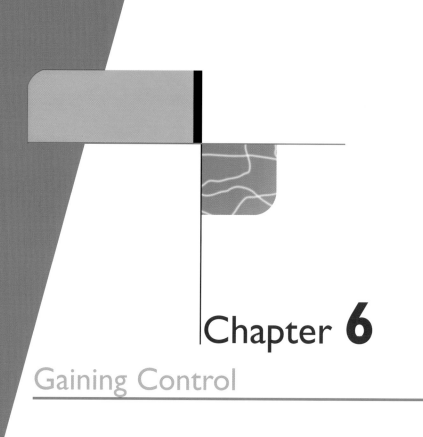

Chapter **6**

Gaining Control

If you're a teen with ADHD, you know what it's like to feel out of control. One teen said that ADHD is like driving a car with no brakes. Until now, parents, teachers, and other adults may have put the brakes on your behavior. You're at a point in your life, however, when you need to take control. Your ADHD should not be an excuse for bad behavior or poor performance. You can do many things to assume more responsibility for managing your ADHD.

It's possible to turn negatives into positives. For example, being stubborn could instead be viewed as being persistent. Here are more examples:

Negative	Positive
Lazy	Laid back
Impulsive	Willing to try new things
Bossy	Good leader
Can't follow directions	Creative thinker
Argumentative	Independent thinker

Develop a Positive Attitude

Feeling good about yourself and believing in yourself are essential for gaining control of your life. Remember, qualities that may be negative in a school setting may be positive in the working world. For example, hyperactivity may give a person energy to handle several projects at once. Being willing to make quick decisions and take risks is a plus in many jobs. Ask your parents, teachers, or therapist to help you identify your strengths.

"I didn't do well in school, and I was often down on myself.

ETHAN, AGE 17

My dad never gave up on me, though. Once, he made me sit down with a piece of paper and a pencil. Together we listed all the things I'm good at and times I've really shined. I put that list on my bulletin board. Now, whenever I feel low I just read that list."

You also can discover your strengths and talents by getting involved in activities at school. Join a club, go out for an individual or team sport, and participate in social events.

Joining a sports team may be a way for some people with ADHD to feel successful.

Get More Involved in Your Treatment

The more involved you are in your own treatment, the more you'll feel in charge. One way to get involved is to learn more about ADHD. Another way is to manage your own medication.

Learn More About ADHD

You need to understand your disability and how it affects you. You can become informed about ADHD in the following ways.

Read about ADHD in books and pamphlets and on the Internet. Look for helpful resources in the For More Information section starting on page 61 of this book.

Talk to professionals who know about ADHD. These people might include a therapist, school nurse, counselor, pediatrician, or special education teacher.

Join an organization that deals with ADHD. Some organizations educate the public, support people and their families, and work for better laws.

Join a support group for teens with ADHD or start one of your own. You'll feel less alone knowing that others share your condition.

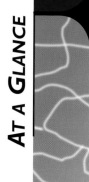
Teens with ADHD tend to forget things. Here are some ways they can remember to take their medication:

- Write a note and stick it on their lunch, desk, or a book.

- Ask a friend to remind them.

- Set their watch or a timer to go off at the right time.

Manage Your Medication

If you take medication as part of your treatment, know your medication and the dosage. Discuss any troublesome side effects with your health care professional. Together, you can find the right medication and dosage.

If you take medication during the school day, know your school's policy on medicines. Your parents may need to sign a consent form. Most likely, the nurse or other school personnel will give you the medication. If so, you might have the person double-check that the prescription is yours and the dosage is correct.

Managing your medication also means taking only the prescribed amount. Don't let classmates or other teens have your pills. Taking someone else's prescription drugs can be dangerous. It's also against the law.

Speak Up for Yourself

When you know about your ADHD, you can be a self-advocate. This means you speak up for yourself. Attend IEP meetings and tell your teachers and parents what you want and what works for you. Be aware of your right to a free and appropriate education. Just because laws exist to protect students with disabilities from discrimination doesn't mean schools will comply automatically. You and your parents may have to request services.

"I started taking karate three years ago. It's really helped my concentration and self-control."
—Nicole, age 13

Tell your teachers about your ADHD and let them know your needs. For example, you might mention you have trouble keeping track of pencils. Ask if you can keep some in class. Your honesty and desire to do well may impress your teachers. They probably will be willing to help. It's best to talk with your teachers at the beginning of each semester rather than waiting for a problem to appear.

Practice Good Health Habits

You'll be in better control of yourself if you feel fit and healthy. Good health habits, along with medication, help to achieve balance in brain chemicals.

Sleep. When you're rested, you're more alert and less likely to miss something important. Teens with ADHD who take medication may have sleep problems. They may not be able to get to sleep, or they may feel sleepy all the time. Adjusting your medication may solve sleep problems.

Diet. A healthy diet helps you stay sharp and focused. Eating regularly can help eliminate stomachaches and headaches that sometimes are a side effect of medication.

Exercise. Exercise helps burn off extra energy and control feelings of restlessness. You'll feel less fidgety and be able to sit still longer.

Relationships with friends may suffer if someone with ADHD has poor social skills. Ask your family and friends for their support in learning to be a good friend.

Work on Your Impulsiveness

Impulsiveness can cause problems for teens with ADHD. Two big problem areas are relationships and driving.

Relationships

Teens with ADHD may blurt out statements that hurt the feelings of other people. They may interrupt others or take over a conversation. Sometimes they change their plans unexpectedly and leave friends waiting and wondering. Such behavior can have a negative effect on friendships and dating.

If impulsiveness is hurting your relationships, you need to take control. You might join clubs or groups where you can practice interacting with others. Support groups for teens with ADHD often teach social skills. Ask your parents and friends for help. They can let you know how you're doing.

ADD and ADHD

Impulsive behavior can lead to poor driving decisions. Teens with ADHD need to take extra precautions.

Driving

Being able to drive a car is a top priority for most teens. This can be dangerous for teens with ADHD. If you want a driver's license, you'll need to take extra precautions. Taking driver's education is absolutely essential. If medication helps you remain calm and focused, you must take it before getting behind the wheel. Even after you get your license, continue driving with an adult in the car until you gain more experience. If you can't trust yourself to drive safely, you may decide not to get your license for now.

Points to Consider

What are your strengths? Make a list.

Why might teens with ADHD not want to take medication at school?

What should a teen tell friends about his or her ADHD?

How could a teen's impulsiveness lead to trouble?

More than half of teens with ADHD continue to experience symptoms as adults. Symptoms, however, may be less severe than in childhood. Adults with ADHD usually learn ways to cope with their condition.

ADHD in adults is diagnosed and treated in much the same way as ADHD in teens.

Modifying the workplace can help adults with ADHD be successful in a job or career. It's a good idea for adults with ADHD to choose a career that fits their disorder.

Teens with ADHD can begin planning now for a job or career. This includes finding out about different jobs and identifying their skills and interests. Making a transition plan will help teens with ADHD move toward independence.

Research continues into the causes of ADHD and ways to treat it. The future looks hopeful for people with ADHD.

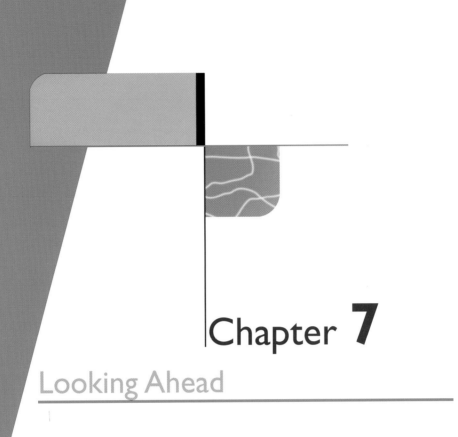

Chapter **7**

Looking Ahead

Teens with ADHD may wonder, "Will I be like this for the rest of my life?" More than half of teens with ADHD will continue to have symptoms as adults. The symptoms, however, may change or decrease. Teens who receive proper diagnosis and treatment will be better able to cope with their ADHD as adults.

Adults and ADHD

It's been recognized only recently that ADHD can be a lifelong condition. More research on ADHD in adults is needed.

Job-related accidents cost employers millions of dollars each year. Employees with undiagnosed ADHD may cause many of these accidents.

At present, treatment for adults with ADHD is much the same as treatment for teens. This includes the use of Ritalin and other stimulant drugs, although adults may need higher dosages. Diagnosis usually occurs when the adult enters therapy for depression, substance abuse, anger management, or another problem. Adults may recognize symptoms of ADHD in themselves when a son or daughter is being diagnosed. It's important to involve family members in an adult's treatment, especially the person's husband or wife.

Choosing a Career

If you're a teen with ADHD, you can begin to plan for a job or career now. Junior high or middle school students can explore different careers. They can read books, attend career fairs, and talk with people in the community. Tests are available to help teens learn about their job interests and skills. Teens can discuss their test results with a school counselor.

High school students should continue to learn about different careers and assess their capabilities. They can take classes related to their fields of interest. A part-time job, an internship, or volunteering are other ways to learn about careers.

"When I was in junior high, I needed help with reading and

math. The special ed teacher asked me to be a 'Monroe Tutor.' Twice a week, we went to nearby Monroe Elementary School and tutored first- and second-graders in reading and math. That's when I found out that I have a talent for working with little kids. I really enjoyed it. Now I want to get a teaching degree after I graduate from high school."

Education After High School

Most well-paying, interesting jobs require some type of education beyond high school. After high school, you may need to earn a degree or certificate to enter the career of your choice. This means taking classes at a vocational or technical school, community college, or university.

The idea of more schooling may not appeal to you. Many young people with ADHD, however, do better in a post-high-school program than they did in high school. They have fewer classes to attend, and they usually take classes that interest them. Rather than sitting at a desk all day, students may have more opportunities to be active.

An important part of career planning is to investigate schools after high school. Write for their catalogs and visit their campuses. Find out if the school can accommodate your special needs. For example, ask if study programs or tutors are available. Remember, the Rehabilitation Act requires public colleges and universities to modify teaching methods and materials for students with disabilities.

DID YOU KNOW?

It's possible for high school students with ADHD to take the Scholastic Aptitude Test (SAT) untimed. A student's score on the SAT may determine whether or not he or she gets into college.

Part of your preparation is making a transition plan. This gives actions or steps to help you move from high school to a job or college. If you receive services under the IDEA, your IEP must state which transition services you will need. The services include things such as career counseling and instruction in independent living skills. Families and school professionals help to write the transition plan.

Preparing for Independence

One day, you'll graduate from high school and leave home for college or a job. Your family members may worry that you won't be able to manage on your own. They may wonder how you'll get along without their constant reminding. You may wonder about this, too. You can start now to take steps toward independence.

One way is to ask for more responsibility at home and then show that you can handle it. For example, volunteer to make dinner. Then have your mom or dad make a checklist of steps for you to follow. Hold a family meeting to establish house rules such as curfew time. Then show that you can be home on time. Work out a contract for doing household chores. Then design a system of notes, lists, or beepers to remind yourself to get a job done.

Find out all you can when you check out colleges or other schools to attend after high school. The future looks bright for people with ADHD.

To the Future

Much progress has been made recently to improve the quality of life of people with ADHD and their families. Research continues into the causes of ADHD and ways to prevent it. Studies also are underway to determine the best methods of treatment. Teens with ADHD can look forward to the future.

Points to Consider

Name some jobs or careers that might suit a person with ADHD. What jobs or careers might be unsuitable?

In what ways might a teen with ADHD benefit from a part-time or summer job?

How could you learn more about education following high school?

Glossary

accommodation (uh-kom-uh-DAY-shuhn)—something supplied to meet a need

bipolar disorder (BYE-poh-luhr diss-OR-dur)—a condition marked by extreme mood swings

diagnose (dye-uhg-NOHSS)—to determine an illness

hyperactive (hye-pur-AK-tiv)—tending to be more active than usual or desired

impulsive (im-PUHL-siv)—tending to act without thinking

inattentive (in-uh-TEN-tiv)—tending not to listen or pay attention; easily distracted.

nausea (NAW-zee-uh)—upset stomach

neurobiological (nu-roh-bye-oh-LOJ-i-kuhl)—relating to the interaction of the nervous system and body chemistry

neurologist (nu-ROL-uh-jist)—a doctor who specializes in disorders of the nervous system

neurotransmitter (nu-roh-transs-MIT-ur)—a chemical that the brain produces and that moves messages along nerve cells

psychiatrist (sye-KYE-uh-trist)—a medical doctor trained to diagnose and treat mental illness

psychologist (sye-KOL-uh-jist)—a person who provides testing and counseling to people with mental and emotional problems

self-esteem (SELF ess-TEEM)—a feeling of personal pride and self-respect

For More Information

Connelly, Elizabeth Russell. *Conduct Unbecoming: Hyperactivity, Attention Deficit, and Disruptive Behavior Disorders*. Philadelphia: Chelsea House, 1999.

Crist, James. *ADHD: A Teenager's Guide*. King of Prussia, PA: Center for Applied Psychology, 1996.

Ingersoll, Barbara D. *Distant Drums, Different Drummers: A Guide for Young People With ADHD*. Bethesda, MD: Cape Publications, 1995.

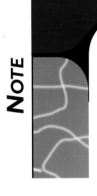

NOTE

At publication, all resources listed here were accurate and appropriate to the topics covered in this book. Addresses and phone numbers may change. When visiting Internet sites and links, use good judgment. Remember, never give personal information over the Internet.

Useful Addresses and Internet Sites

Children and Adults With Attention Deficit/Hyperactivity Disorder (CHADD) Canada
1376 Bank Street
Ottawa, ON K1H 1B3
CANADA
www.chaddcanada.org

Children and Adults With Attention-Deficit/Hyperactivity Disorder (CHADD)
8181 Professional Place, Suite 201
Landover, MD 20785
1-800-233-4050
www.chadd.org

National Attention Deficit Disorder Association (ADDA)
1788 Second Street, Suite 200
Highland Park, IL 60035
www.add.org

National Information Center for Children and Youth With Disabilities (NICHCY)
PO Box 1492
Washington, DC 20013-1492
1-800-695-0285
www.nichcy.org

About.Com ADD
http://add.about.com/health/add/mbody.htm
Many links organized by topic

Index

ADD. *See* ADHD
ADHD
    causes of, 9, 11–15
    controlling, 47–53
    diagnosis of, 9, 19–26, 55, 56
    symptoms of, 5, 6, 19, 20, 21, 26,
        27, 31, 35, 55
    treatment of, 19, 22, 24, 31–37,
        49–50, 55, 59
    types of, 22
    who has it, 6
adults and ADHD, 55–59
alcohol abuse, 8, 15, 19, 56
alternative therapies, 37
American Medical Association
    (AMA), 26
American Psychiatric Association
    (APA), 21
anger, 16, 35, 36, 41, 56
antidepressants, 32
anxiety, 16, 20
attitude, 48

behavior modification, 34
biofeedback, 24
bipolar disorder, 16, 20
brain, 12, 13, 14, 15, 16, 17, 23, 24,
    32, 33
brain chemicals, 14, 33, 51

careers, 56
Centers for Disease Control and
    Prevention (CDC), 26
classrooms, 42–43
coaching, 14, 34, 36
concentration, 20, 26, 33, 43

control, 47, 53
counseling, 23, 31, 34–35. *See also*
    school counselors

depression, 8, 16, 17, 20, 35, 56
diet, 37, 51
directions, 42
disabilities, 7, 17, 40, 41, 50, 57
distractions, 43
dopamine, 32
driving, 47, 53
drug abuse, 8, 15, 19, 56
drug therapy, 33

education, 31, 34, 39. *See also* school
    post high school, 57–58
environment, 31, 36, 42. *See also*
    home; school; work
    environment

family, 6, 8, 11, 17, 31, 35, 44, 48, 52,
    56, 58, 59
504 Accommodation Plan, 40
flexibility, 42
friends, 8, 52

head injuries, 12, 13
health care professionals, 23, 24, 26,
    35, 48, 49, 50
health habits, 51
heredity, 15
home, 11, 12, 21, 35, 36, 44
hyperactivity, 6, 8, 11, 12, 14, 22, 25,
    26, 28, 32, 36, 48

Index continued